Dave Matthews Band

crash

Transcribed by Jeff Jacobson and Paul Pappas

Cover Illustration by Thane Kerner
Band photography by C. Taylor Crothers

 For a comprehensive listing of Cherry Lane Music's songbooks, sheet music,
instructional materials, videos and more, check out our entire catalog on the Internet.
Our home page address is: http://www.cherrylane.com

One of pop's most striking recent success stories has been the rise of the Dave Matthews Band, whose major-label debut *Under The Table And Dreaming* was praised by *Rolling Stone* as "one of the most ambitious releases of '94." The album has sold over four million copies, and earned two Grammy nominations for the first single, "What Would You Say."

The band was destined for such a breakthrough, with or without a Top 40 hit, thanks to its feverish grassroots support and the group's own unique talent. Dubbed "unpeggable and totally addictive" by *Details*, the Dave Matthews Band stood out from the horde of would-be alternatives with one of the most original sounds to emerge in the '90s.

Now the band is poised to break down more doors with *Crash*, its highly anticipated second RCA album. "It's way more aggressive, way more sexy, way softer and way louder," says frontman Dave Matthews. For all its extremes, however, the diverse elements of Matthews' hypnotic voice and acoustic guitar, Boyd Tinsley's Cajun-spry violin, Leroi Moore's shy R&B sax, Stefan Lessard's funk-fluid bass, and Carter Beauford's power-jazz drums are broadened and blended into a more integrated, accessible form. From the funk-wound nerve of the first single, "Too Much," to the lusty ripples of "Crash Into Me," the Dave Matthews Band only sound more like itself.

Matthews credits producer Steve Lillywhite (U2, Talking Heads, Rolling Stones) with a relaxed, yet adventurous attitude in the studio. All band members played together to record the basic tracks. "We were more or less in a circle where we could all see each other," Matthews says of the sessions. "That makes this album a lot more in the spirit of how we play on stage."

There was a good deal of experimentation in the studio, too. Lessard brought a six-string and an acoustic bass into the mix. Moore added some funky baritone sax riffing to his arsenal, which he laid upon the other saxophone tracks of "So Much To Say." Moore also featured flute on "Say Goodbye," which opens with an amazing drum roll by Beauford, who contrasts his usual whiplash beats and fills with tasty percussion from congas, cowbells and woodblocks.

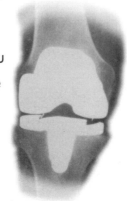

Tinsley also adopts a more textural role on violin, lacing "Two Step" with plucky pizzicato lines, while serving a familiar rustic rave-up in "Tripping Billies." That song, its name inspired by a girlfriend who said it sounded like "hillbillies on acid," was first heard on the group's self-released live debut, *Remember Two Things* (which has sold 350,000 copies since its 1993 release), but lost nothing in studio translation. "Boyd would start sawing away on his violin, and we were screaming and dancing and clapping around behind him," Matthews says of the new version. "When I hear that solo, it holds a big memory for me."

Indeed, the momentum and moods throughout much of *Crash* are the stuff of memories and hindsight, from the hairpin grooves of "Drive In Drive Out" to resonate low songs like "Let You Down." The sense that we are all primates—with simple goals cast to destiny—surfaces in the closing track, "Proudest Monkey," which Matthews relates to his own humble start as a bartender in Charlottesville, Virginia. "When the song started out, it was about how we people have sort of left, or at least like to think that we've left the woods," he says. "But I'm proud of the position that we've moved into."

Contents

Left to right: Leroi Moore (saxophones), Boyd Tinsley (violin), Carter Beauford (drums/percussion), Stefan Lessard (bass), Dave Matthews (guitar/vocals)

So Much To Say

Words and Music by David Matthews,
Boyd Tinsley and Peter Griesar

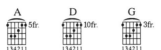

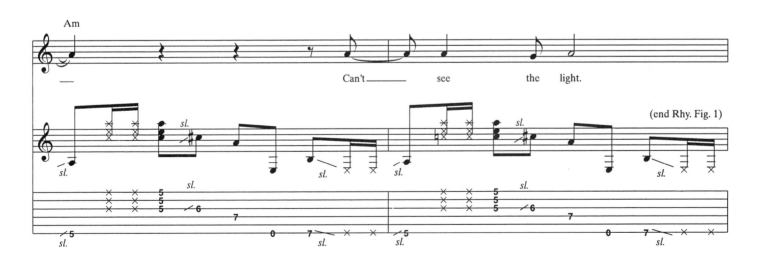

w/Rhy. Fig. 1 (5 times)

And my heav-en is a nice house____ in the sky.____ Got cen-tral heat-ing

and I'm al - right.____ Yeah, yeah,____ yeah,____

____ can't____ see the light. Keep it____ locked up in - side.____

____ Don't talk____ a - bout it.____ T - T - Talk a - bout the weath-er.____

(Band in)

Yeah, yeah,____ yeah,____

*Riff A (**Gtr. II)

* Play w/slight variations ad lib. when recalled (throughout).
** Elec. w/clean tone

____ can't____ see the light.

(end Riff A)

sl.

sl.

(Resume Riff A)

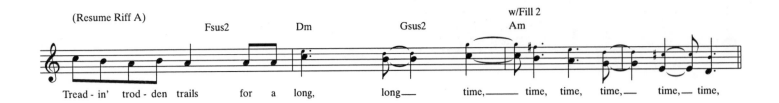

Fsus2   Dm   Gsus2   w/Fill 2 Am

Tread - in' trod - den trails   for a long,   long——   time,—— time, time, time,—— time,—— time,

Bridge

A   D

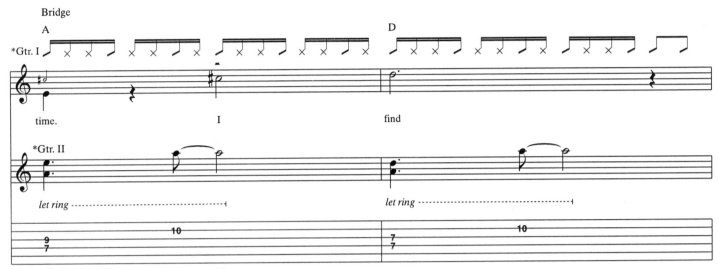

time.   I   find

*Gtr. II

let ring

* 2nd time both gtrs. play w/slight variations ad lib.

G   D

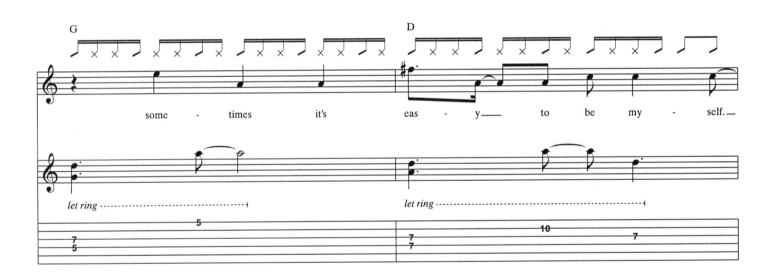

some - times   it's   eas - y —— to be my - self.——

let ring

Fill 2 (Gtr. III)

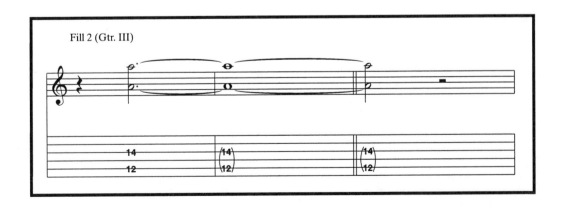

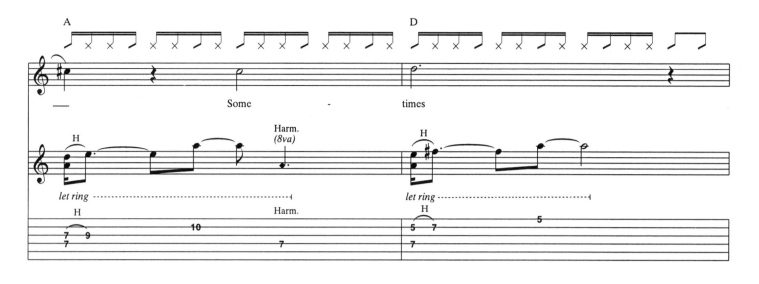

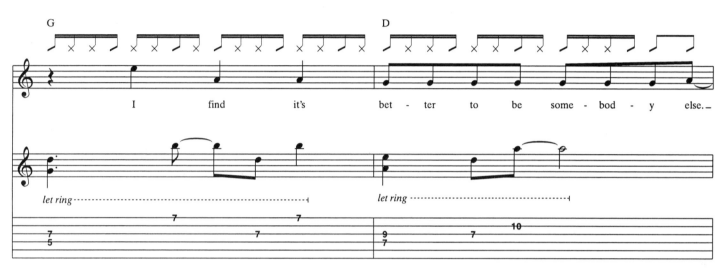

w/Rhy. Fig. 1 and *Riff A (both last 2 bars only)
w/Fill 1

To Coda ⊕

3rd Verse
w/Rhy. Fig. 1 and Riff A (both 4 times)

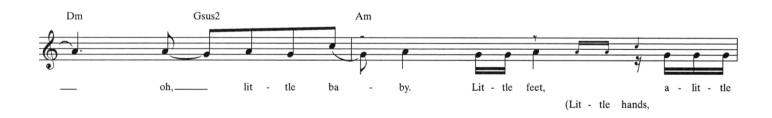

* Gtr. II doubled by Gtr. IV (elec. w/dist. tone) till Coda.

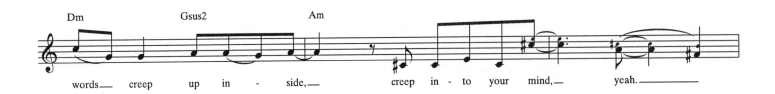

words__ creep up in - side,__ creep in - to your mind,__ yeah.__

w/Fill 1

So much to say, so much__ to say, so much to say, so much__ to say.__

w/Fill 1

D.S. al Coda
%

So much to say, so much__ to say, so much to say, so much__ to say.__ 'Cause

w/Rhy. Fig. 1 (4 times)
w/Riff A (Gtr. II: 4 times; Gtr. IV: 2 times)
w/Fill 1

Coda

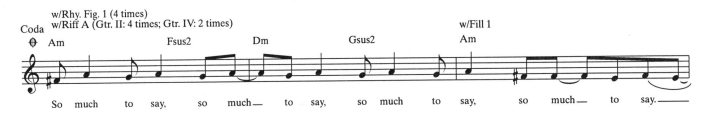

So much to say, so much__ to say, so much to say, so much__ to say.__

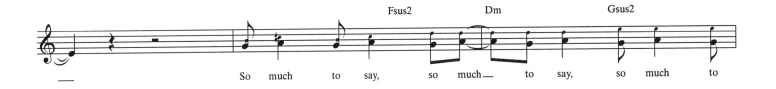

__ So much to say, so much__ to say, so much to

w/Fill 1

say, so much__ to say.__

w/Fill 1

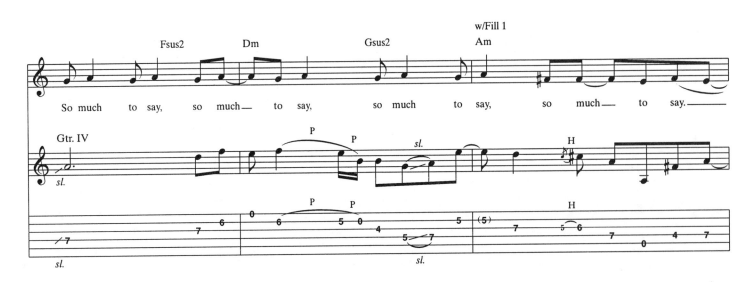

So much to say, so much__ to say, so much to say, so much__ to say.__

Two Step

Words and Music by
David Matthews

Moderately ♩ = 120

*Acous.

*Gtrs. III & IV are acous. w/drop-D tuning: ⑥ = D.

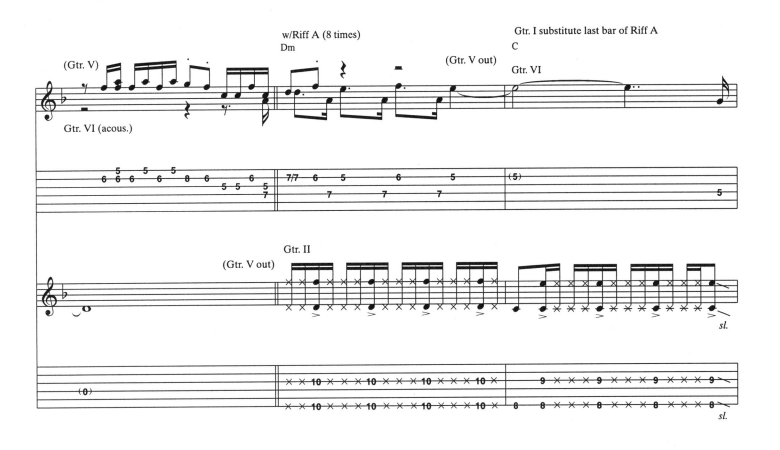

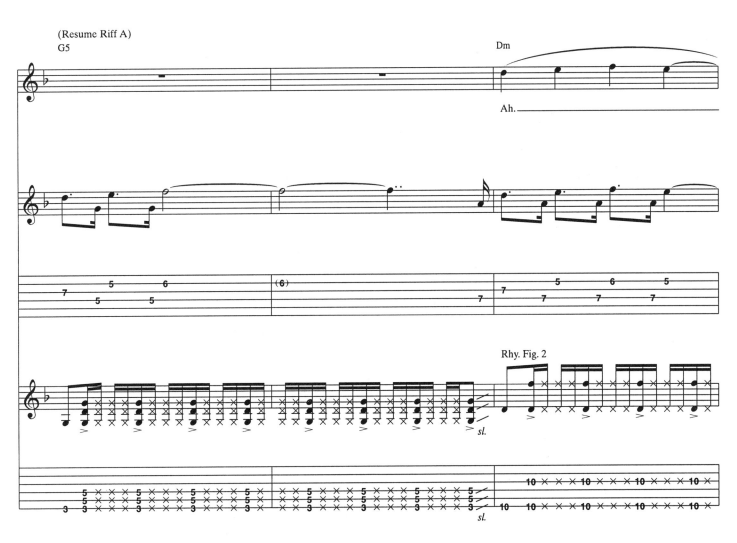

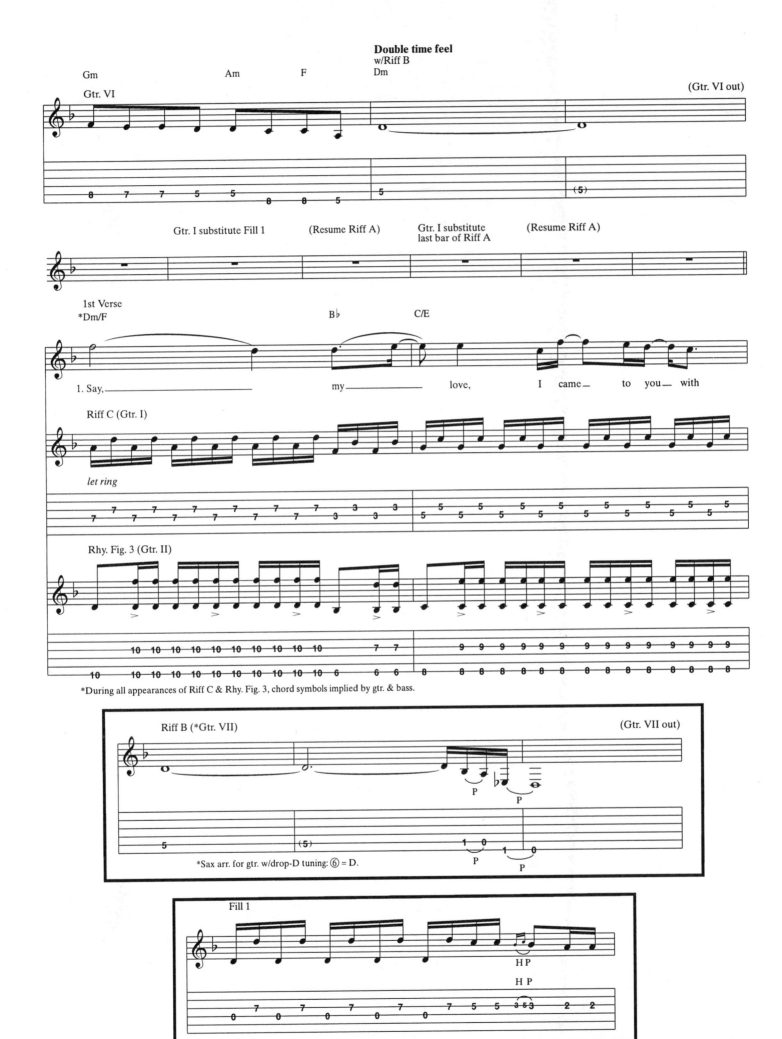

2nd, 3rd, 4th Verses
w/Rhy. Fig. 3 and Riff C (both 2 times)

2. Oh,_____ hey, my__ love, do you__ be - lieve__ that we might__
3.4. *See additional lyrics*

last a_____ thou - sand_____ years or more_ it not_ for

_____ this? Our_____ flesh and_____ blood, it____ ties____

w/Rhy. Fig. 3 and Riff C (both last 2 bars only)   (end double time feel)

_____ you and me_____ right up.___ Tie____ me down. Oh,___

Chorus

_____ well, cel - e - brate__ we__ will,

Riff D (Gtr. I)   (end Riff D)

Rhy. Fig. 4 (Gtr. II)   (end Rhy. Fig. 4)

*Harmony is sung 2nd & 3rd times only. 3rd time harmony includes slight variations ad lib.

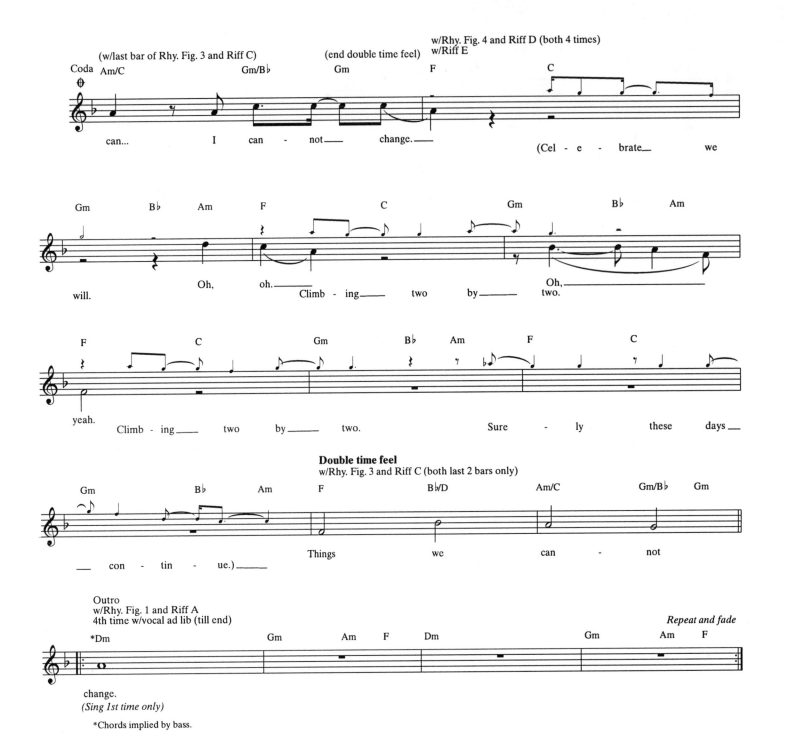

Additional Lyrics

3. Hey, my love, you came to me like
Wine comes to this mouth,
Grown tired of water all the time.
You quench my heart and, oh, you
Quench my mind. *(To Chorus)*

4. Oh, my love, I came to you
With best intentions.
You lay down and give to me
Just what I'm seeking.
Say, love, watch me celebrate. *(To Chorus)*

Crash Into Me

Words and Music by
David Matthews

dream.

2nd, 3rd Verses
w/Rhy. Fig. 1 (2 times)

2. Touch___ your lips just so___ I___ know.___ In___ your eyes, love,___
3. *See additional lyrics*

Additional Lyrics

3. Only if I've gone overboard,
Then I'm begging you
To forgive me, oh,
In my haste.
When I'm holding you so, girl,
Close to me.
Oh, and you come... *(To Chorus)*

Too Much

Words by David Matthews
Music by David Matthews, Carter Beauford,
Stefan Lessard, Leroi Moore and Boyd Tinsley

*Play all repeats and recalled guitar figures w/variations ad lib (throughout)
**Gtr. II to left of slashes.
***Gtr. II is violin arr. for gtr.; Gtr. III is horns arr. for gtr.; Gtr. IV is two gtrs. arr. for one.

*Accented notes are played 1st
time only; omit when recalled.

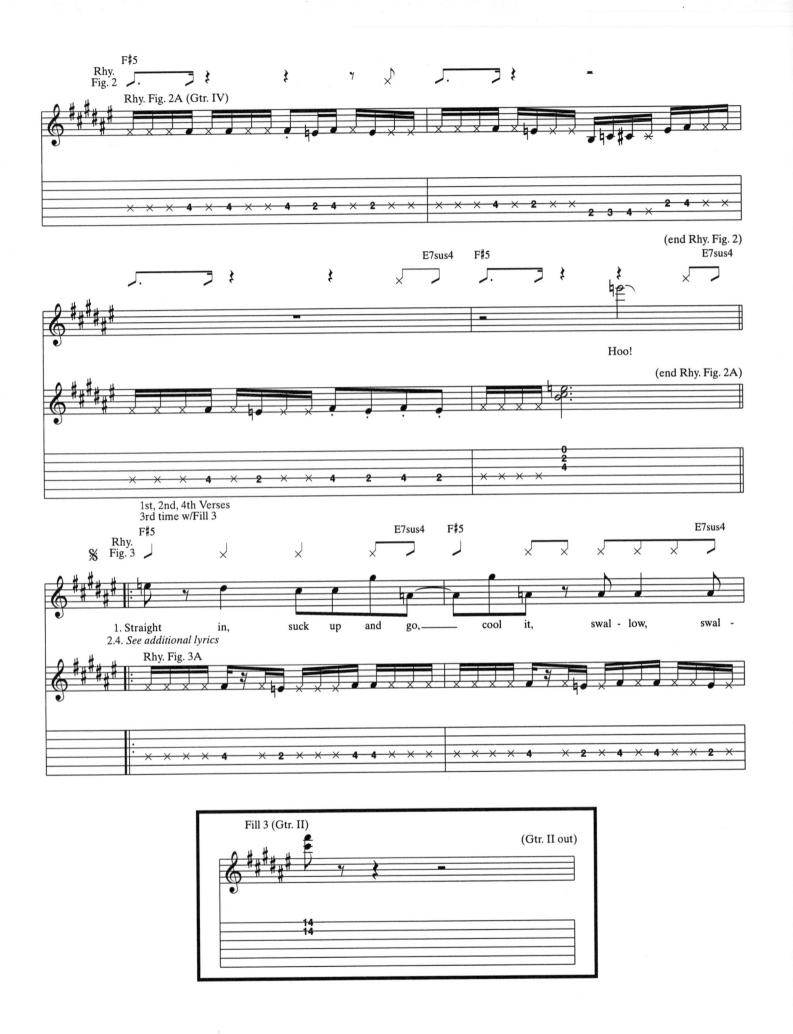

for me, play more, ten times in the same day. I need more.

I'm go-ing o-ver my bor-ders. Gon-na take more, more from you, let-ter by let-ter.

(cont. in slashes)

w/Rhy. Figs. 3 & 3A

38

Additional Lyrics

2. Oh, traffic jam, got more cars than a beach got sand.
   Suck it up, suck it up, suck it up,
   Fill it up until no more.
   I'm no crazy creep.
   I've got it coming to me because I'm not satisfied.
   The hunger keeps on growing. *(To Chorus)*

4. I told God, "I'm coming to your country.
   I'm going to eat up your cities,
   Your homes, you know."
   I've got a stomach full,
   It's not a chip on my shoulder.
   I've got this growl in my tummy
   And I'm gonna stop it today. *(To Chorus)*

#41

Words by David Matthews
Music by David Matthews, Carter Beauford,
Stefan Lessard, Leroi Moore and Boyd Tinsley

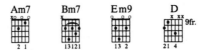

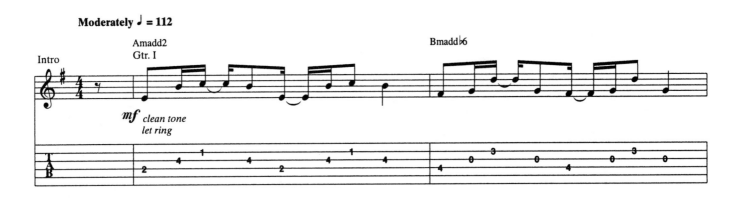

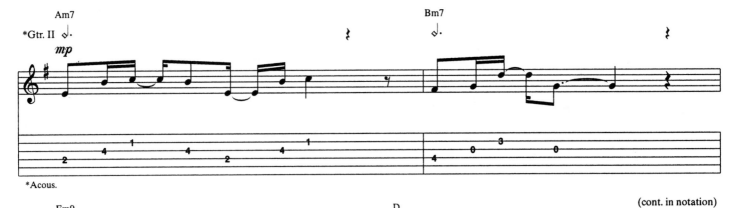

*Acous.

(cont. in notation)

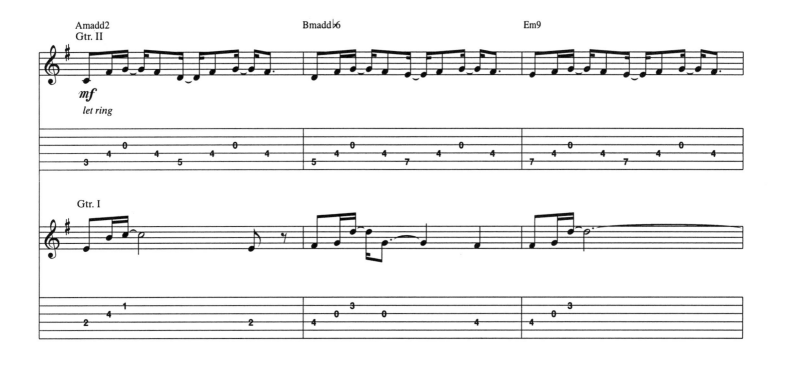

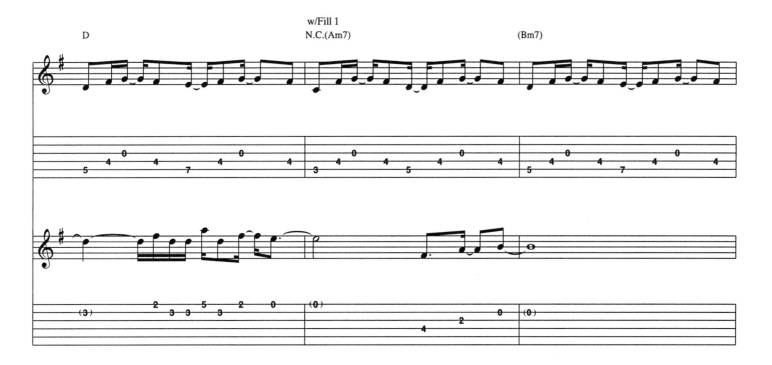

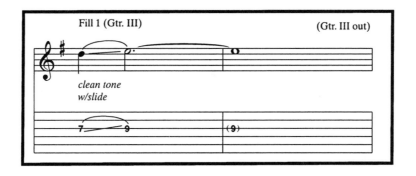

44

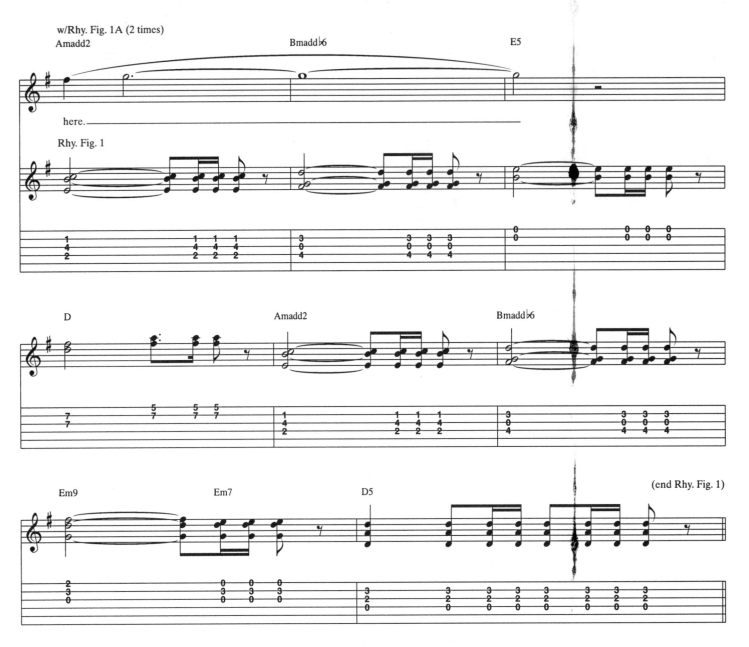

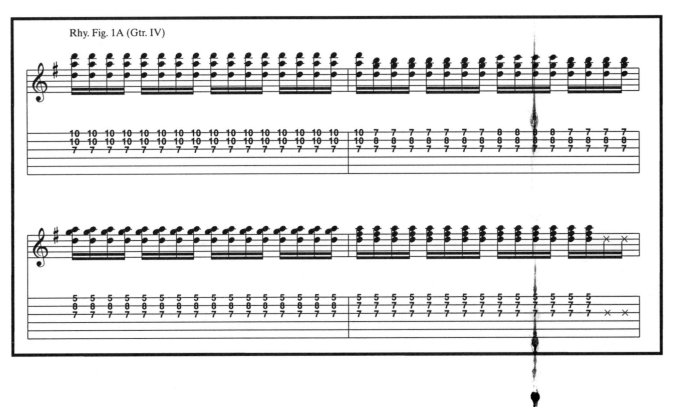

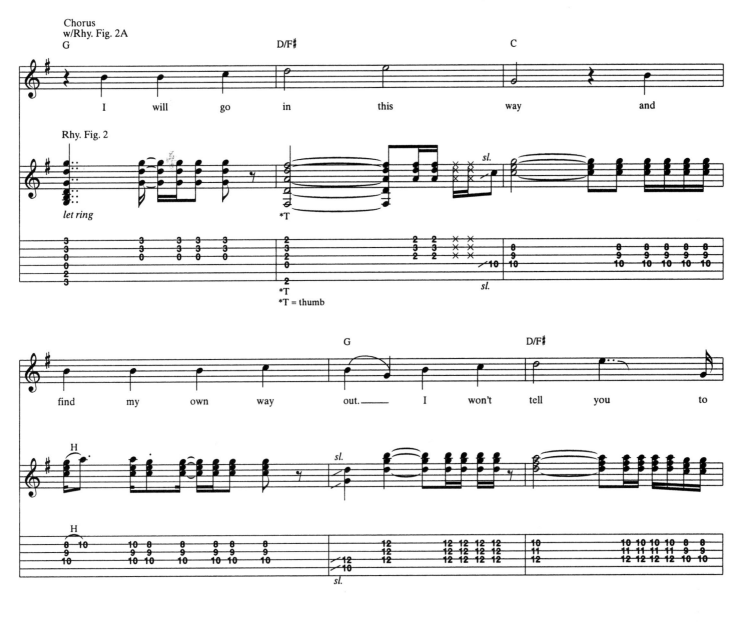

Chorus
w/Rhy. Fig. 2A

I will go in this way and find my own way out.___ I won't tell you to

Rhy. Fig. 2

let ring

*T
*T = thumb

sl.
sl.

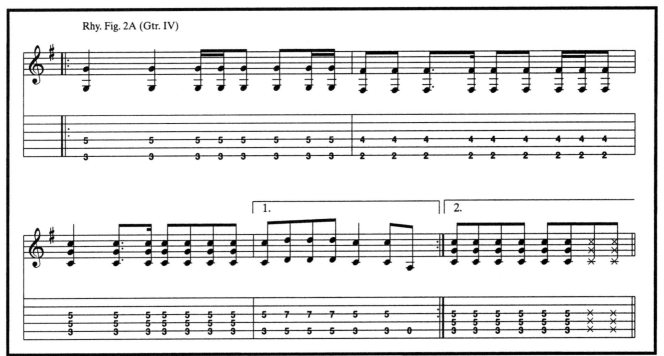

Rhy. Fig. 2A (Gtr. IV)

1.   2.

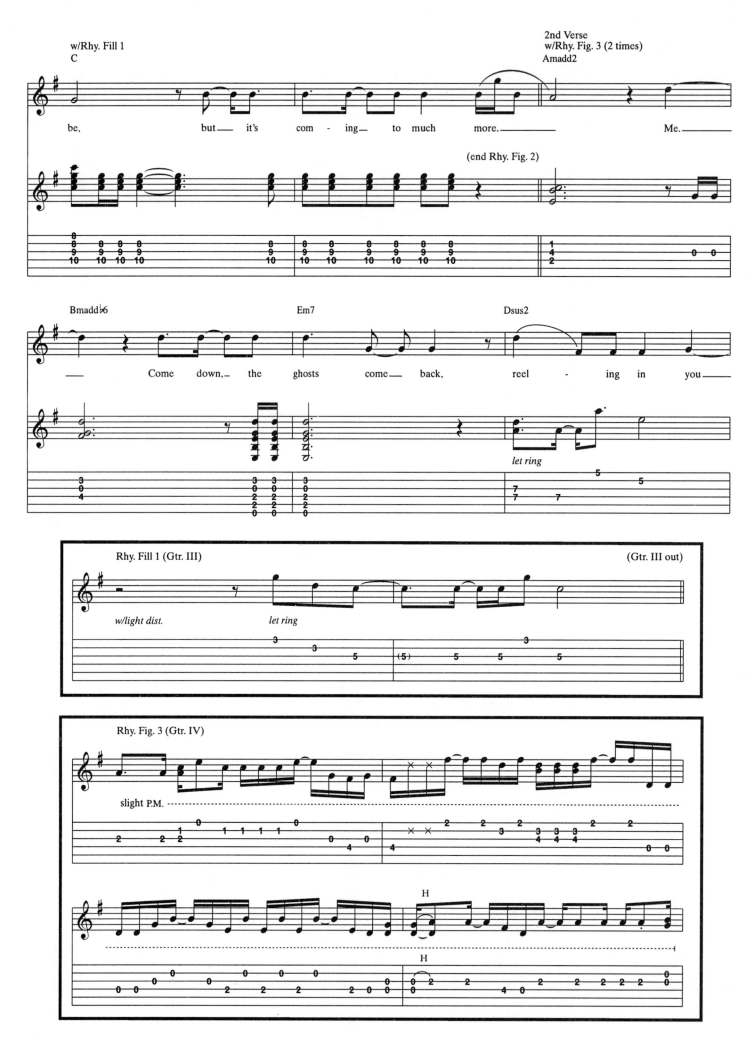

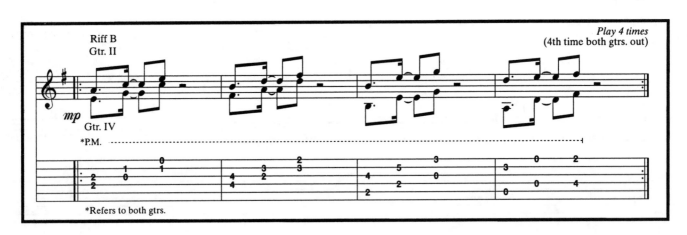

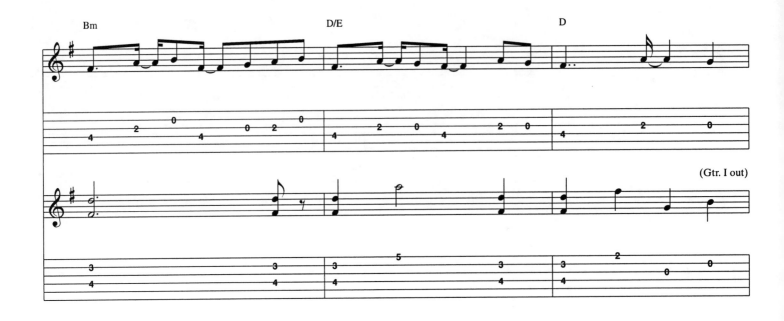

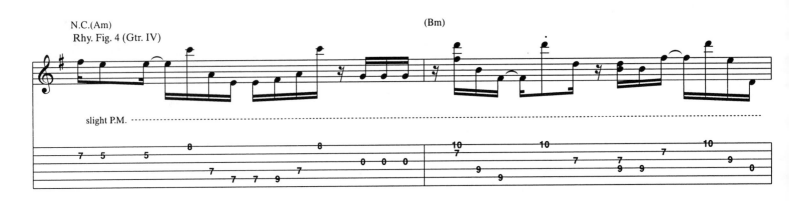

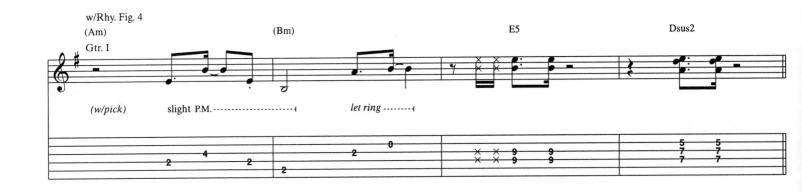

*Play w/slight variations ad lib on repeats.
**Play notes in parentheses 1st time only.

*Chord names indicated by Gtr. IV till end.

Segue to "Say Goodbye"

Say Goodbye

Words and Music by
David Matthews

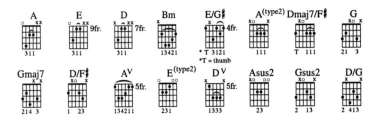

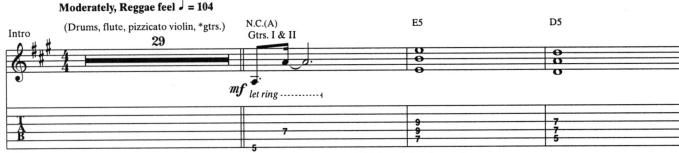

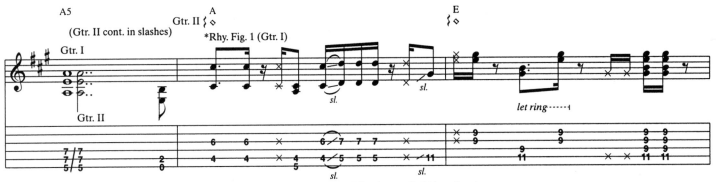

*Gtr. I (acous.) occasionally strums stgs. behind nut (otherwise tacet).
Gtr. II (acous.) strums muted stgs. ad lib.

*Play all rhy. figs. w/slight variations ad lib when recalled (throughout).

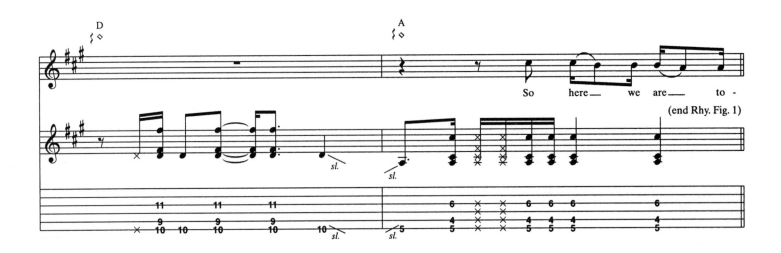

So here— we are— to-

(end Rhy. Fig. 1)

night, you and me to-geth-er with the storm out-

side and the fi-re's bright. Oh, and in your

eyes I see what's on my mind. And you got me wild,

turned a-round in - side. Oh, and then de-si-

re, see, is creep-ing up heav-y, ah, in-side

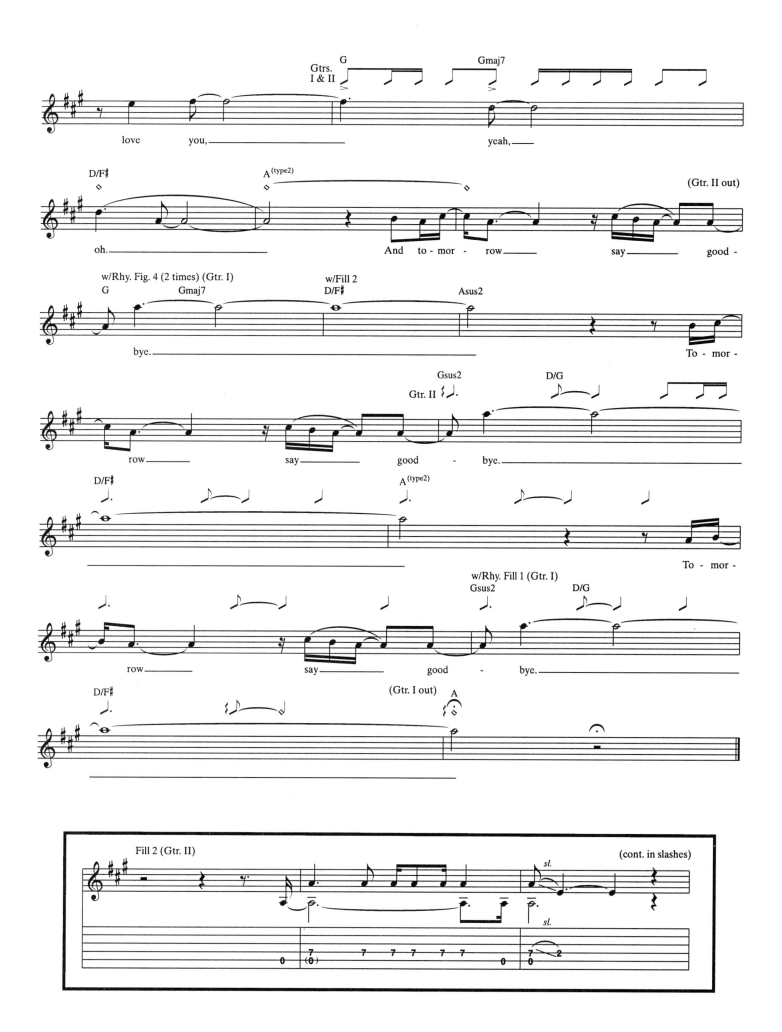

Drive In Drive Out

Words and Music by
David Matthews

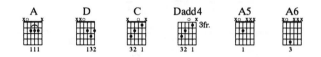

*Play all gtr. figs. w/slight variations ad lib when recalled (throughout).

**Acous.

*Acous.

hear_____ more_____ than I'd___ like to._____ So I

boil_____ my head_____ in a sense of___ hu - mor. I

laugh___ at what I___ can - not___ change._____ And I

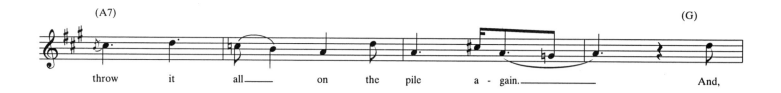

(A7)   (G)

throw   it   all____ on   the   pile   a - gain._____   And,

w/Riff B (4 times)
(A7)   (G)

oh,   when__ I   do   this,__   I ___   do __ it__ for__ you,__   when all__

(A7)   (G)

_____   that   I   want____   is__   so   bad - ly__ to   be___

(A7)   (G)

by_____   my -   self_____   a - gain._____

(A7)   (G)

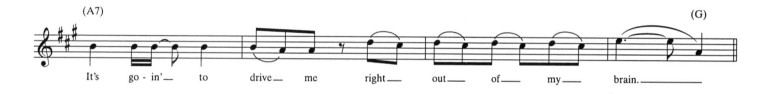

It's   go - in'__ to   drive__ me   right__ out__ of__ my__ brain.___

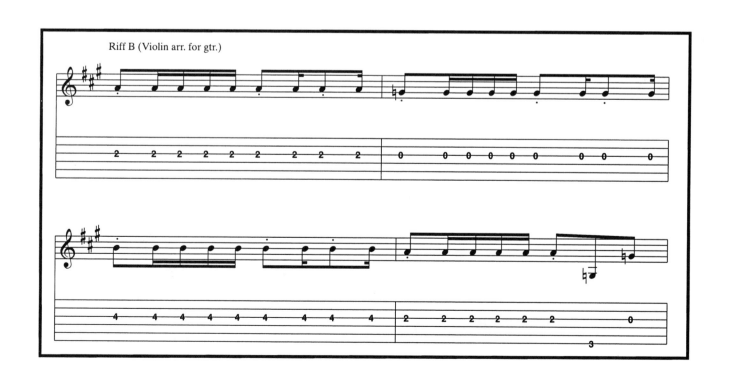

Riff B (Violin arr. for gtr.)

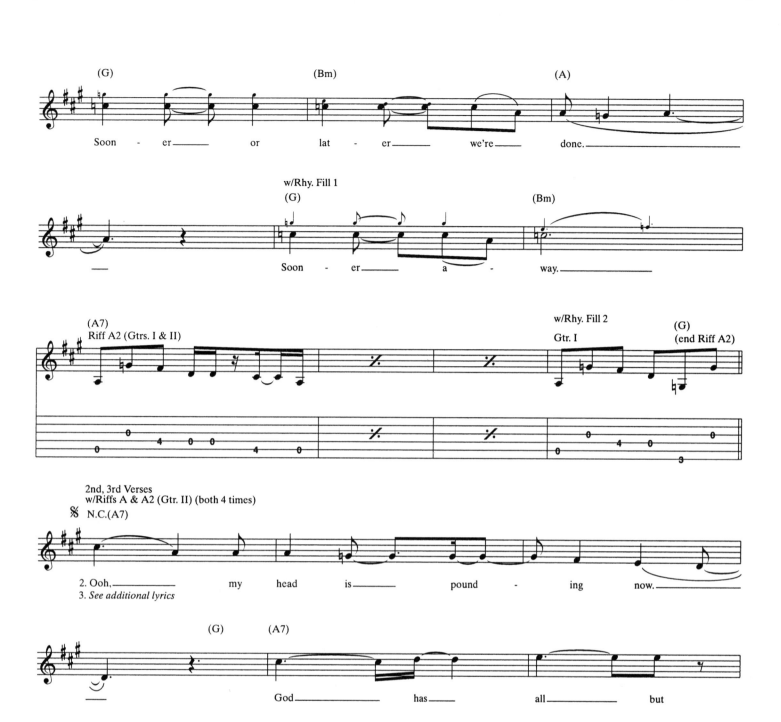

Soon - er ___ or lat - er ___ we're ___ done. ___

w/Rhy. Fill 1

— Soon - er ___ a - way. ___

Riff A2 (Gtrs. I & II)

w/Rhy. Fill 2
Gtr. I
(end Riff A2)

2nd, 3rd Verses
w/Riffs A & A2 (Gtr. II) (both 4 times)

N.C.(A7)

2. Ooh, ___ my head is ___ pound - ing now. ___
3. *See additional lyrics*

God ___ has ___ all ___ but

left ___ me be - hind. ___ Not ___

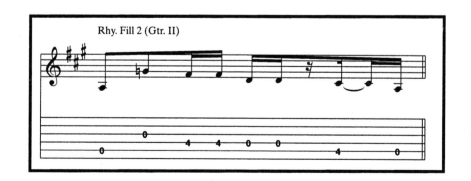

Rhy. Fill 2 (Gtr. II)

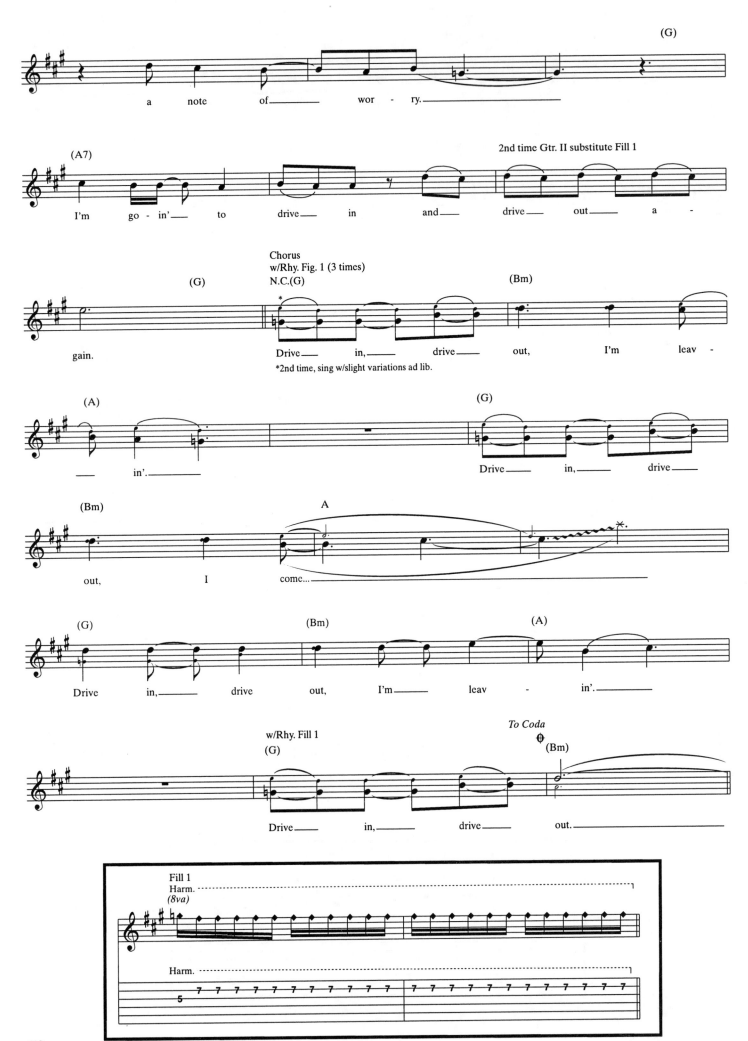

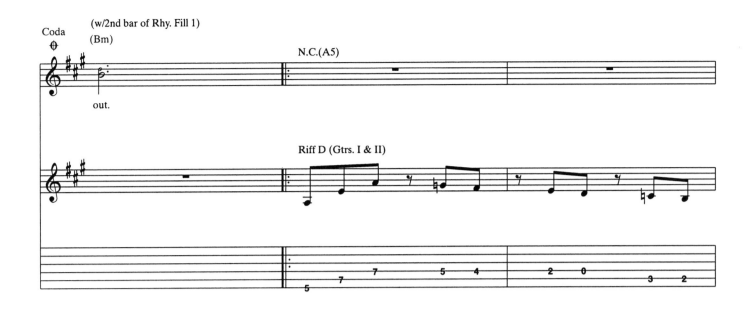

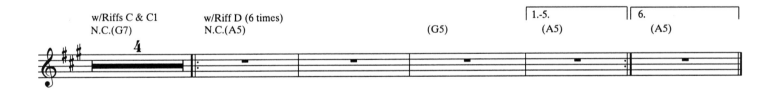

Additional Lyrics

3. Here, oh, I'm over this arrangement.
   Around here, oh, emptiness sounded so good.
   I want to drive you right into my world. *(To Chorus)*

Let You Down

Words by David Matthews
Music by David Matthews and Stefan Lessard

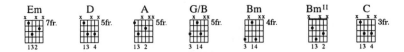

*Two acous. gtrs. arr. for one

*Omit ties when Riff B
 is recalled.

*Sound all notes w/vol. knob swells (till end).

(*Sax enters)

*Whistling ends.

w/Rhy. Fig. 1 & Riff A

Repeat and fade

*Gtr. IV

Gtr. III

*Elec. w/dist. tone. Sound all notes w/vol. knob swells (till end).
**Play beat 1 1st time only; tacet on repeats.

Additional Lyrics

3. I let you down.
    How could I be such a fool like me?
    I let you down.
    Tail between my legs.
    I'm a puppy for your love.
    I'm a puppy for your love. *(To Chorus)*

Lie In Our Graves

Words by David Matthews
Music by David Matthews, Carter Beauford,
Stefan Lessard, Leroi Moore and Boyd Tinsley

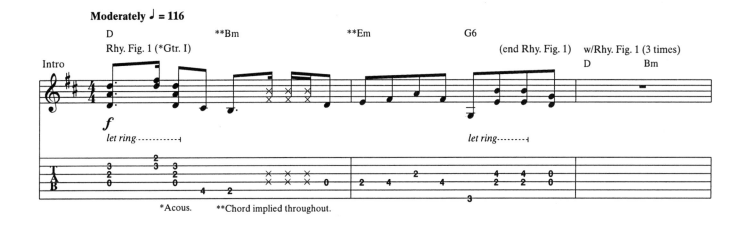

*Acous. **Chord implied throughout.

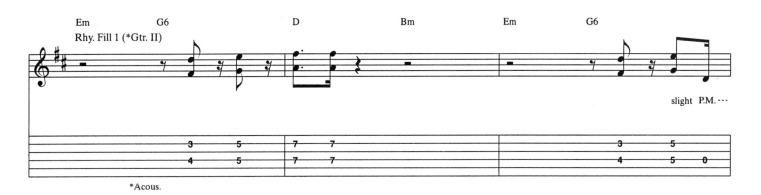

*Acous.

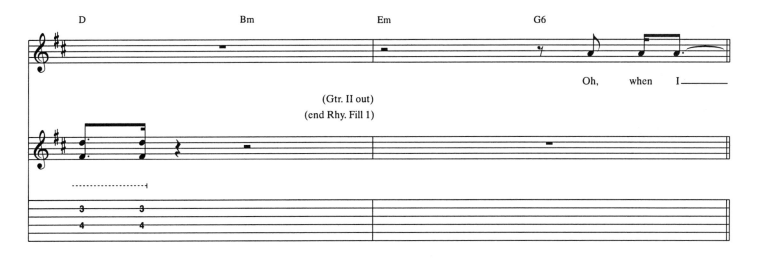

(Gtr. II out)
(end Rhy. Fill 1)

Oh,   when   I

Cry Freedom

Words and Music by
David Matthews

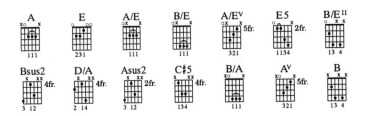

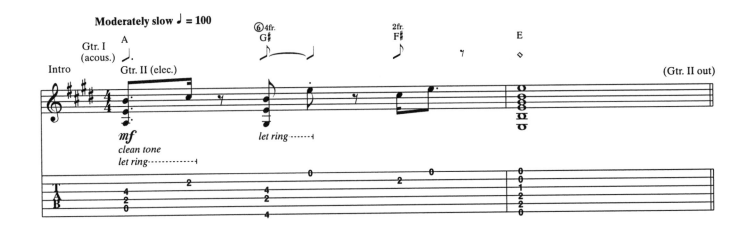

How can I turn a-way?___ Broth-er, Sis-ter, go danc-ing through my head,___

___ hu-man___ as to___ hu-man. The fu-

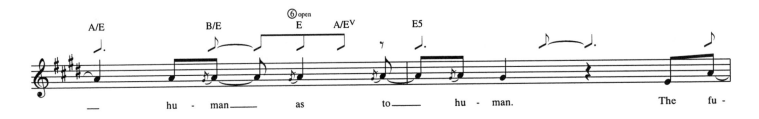

ture is___ no place to place your___ bet-ter___ days.

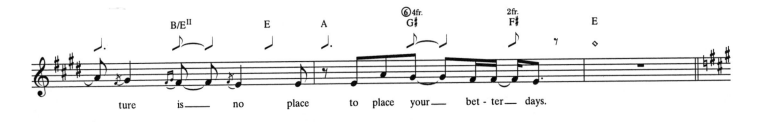

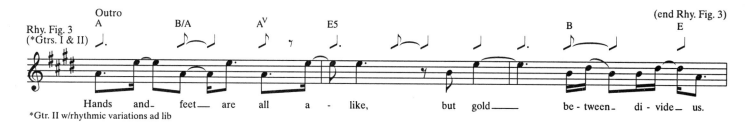

Outro

Rhy. Fig. 3
(*Gtrs. I & II)

(end Rhy. Fig. 3)

Hands and_ feet_ are all a - like, but gold____ be - tween_ di - vide_ us.

*Gtr. II w/rhythmic variations ad lib

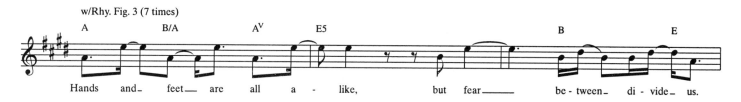

w/Rhy. Fig. 3 (7 times)

Hands and_ feet_ are all a - like, but fear____ be - tween_ di - vide_ us.

Hands and_ feet are____ all____ a - like, yeah.____ Hear what I____ say.____

____ Hear what I say. Oh,____ so be it,____ yeah.____ I wan-na dance a -

w/Fill 1

way,____ yeah,____ ba ba ba.

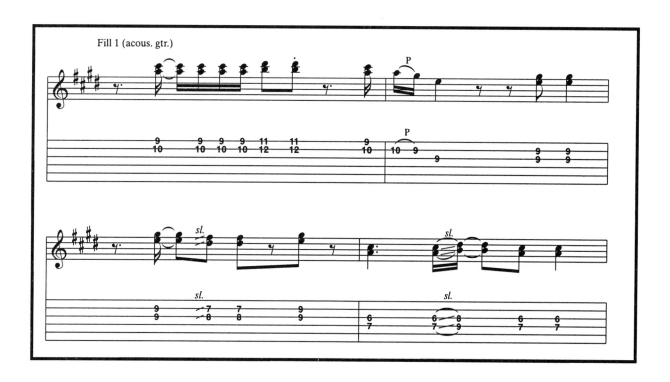

Fill 1 (acous. gtr.)

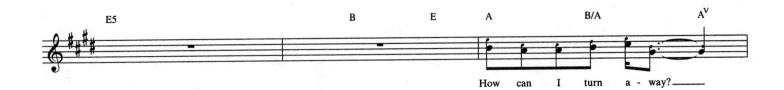

How can I turn a - way?

Broth - er, Sis - ter, go danc - ing through my head,— hu - man— as to—

— hu - man.— The fu - ture is— no place—

— to place your— bet - ter— days.—

Additional Lyrics

2. There was a window,
And by it stood a mirror
In which he could see himself.
He thought of something,
Something he had never had
But hoped would come along.
Cry freedom, cry,
From deep inside,
Where we are all confined
While we wave hands in fire, yeah. *(To Chorus)*

Tripping Billies

Words and Music by
David Matthews

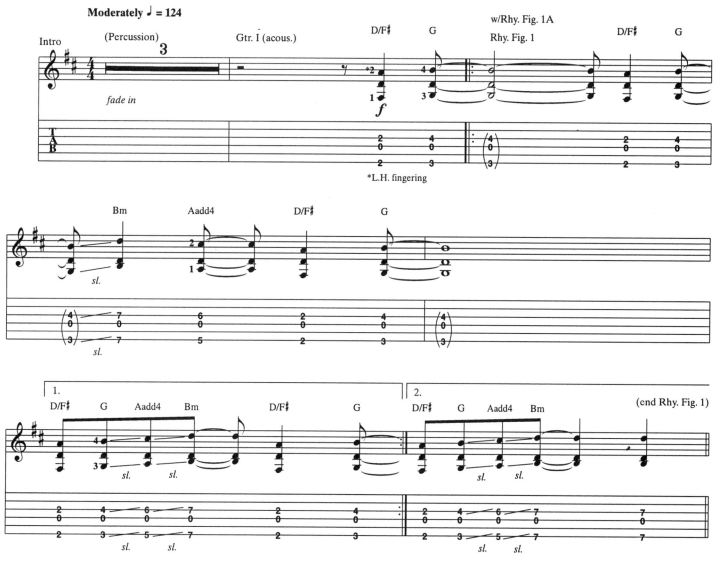

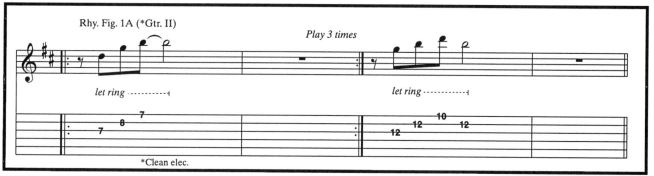

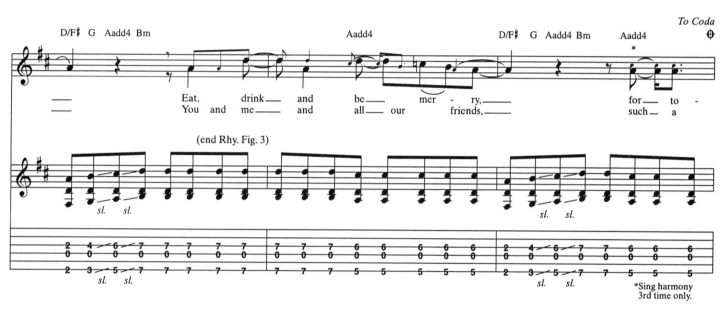

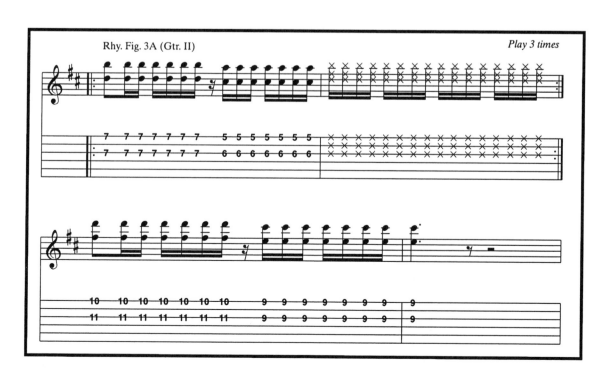

103

Additional Lyrics

2. We're wearing nothing,
   Nothing but our shadows.
   Shadows falling down on the beach sand.
   Remembering once,
   Out on the beaches,
   We wore pineapple grass bracelets. *(To Chorus)*

3. We are all sitting,
   Legs crossed 'round a fire.
   My yellow flame, she dances.
   Tequila drinking,
   Oh, our minds will wander
   To wondrous places. *(To Chorus)*

Proudest Monkey

Words by David Matthews
Music by David Matthews, Carter Beauford,
Stefan Lessard, Leroi Moore and Boyd Tinsley

*Chords implied throughout.

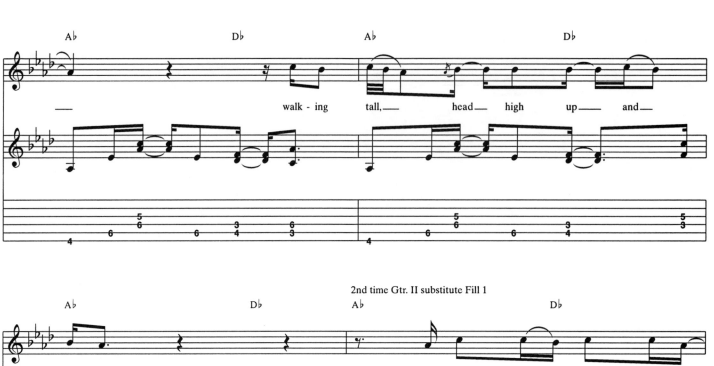

walk - ing   tall,___   head___   high   up___   and___

2nd time Gtr. II substitute Fill 1

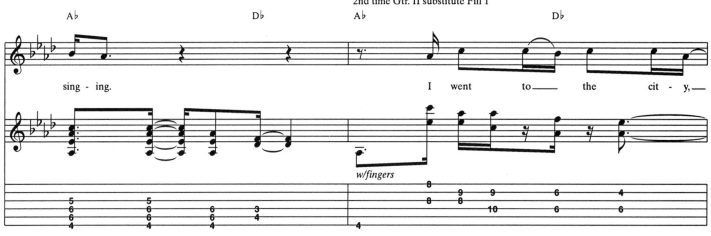

sing - ing.   I   went   to___   the   cit - y,___

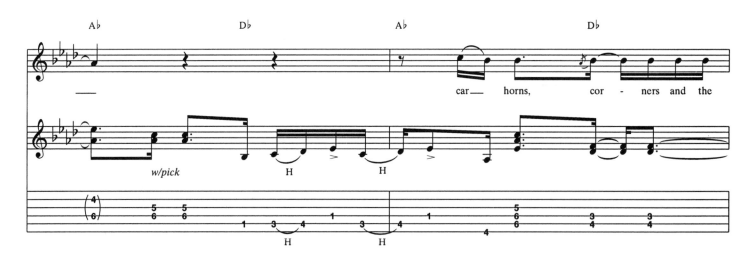

car___   horns,   cor - ners   and   the

w/pick   H   H

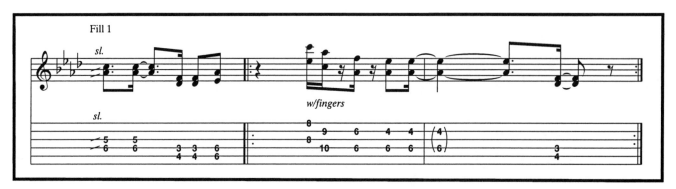

Fill 1

sl.

w/fingers

sl.

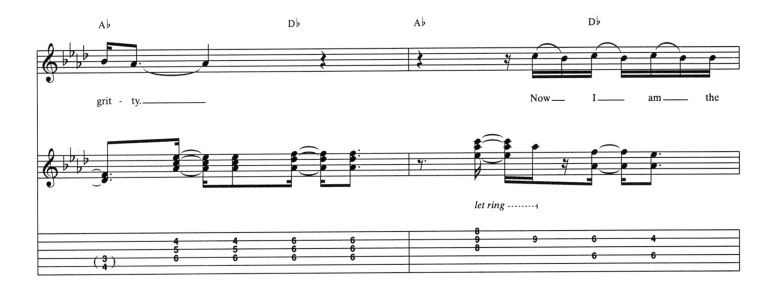

grit - ty._____ Now__ I __ am __ the

let ring ------

proud - est mon - key_____ you've ev - er seen.____

To Coda ⊕

Mon - key see, mon - key do, yeah._____

Guitar solo
w/Rhy. Fig. 1 and *Riff A (both 8 times)

*After 1st time, play w/variations ad lib.

*Played behind the beat.

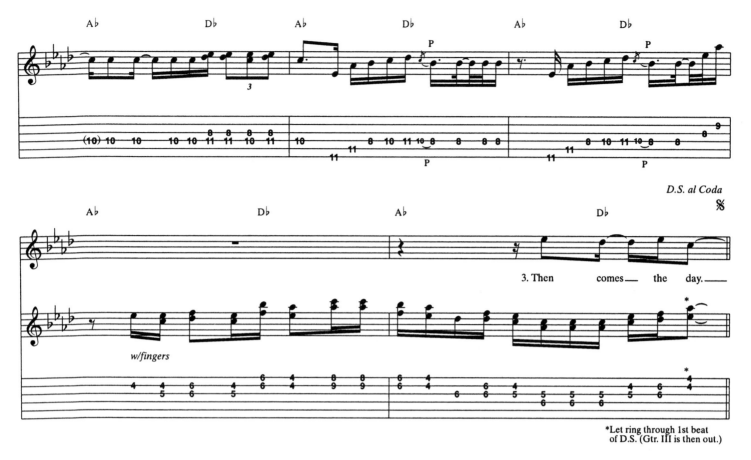

*Let ring through 1st beat
of D.S. (Gtr. III is then out.)

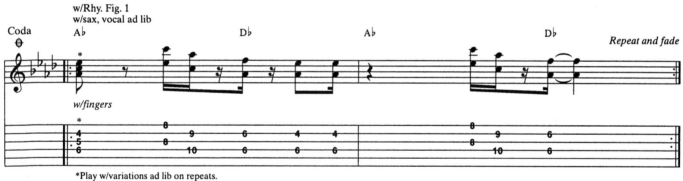

*Play w/variations ad lib on repeats.

Additional Lyrics

3. Then comes the day.
   Staring at myself, I turn
   To question me.
   I wonder, do I want
   The simple, simple life
   That I once lived in well?
   Oh, things were quiet then.
   In a way, they were the better days.
   But now I am the proudest monkey
   You've ever seen.
   Monkey see, monkey do, yeah.

• TABLATURE EXPLANATION/NOTATION LEGEND •

TABLATURE: A six-line staff that graphically represents the guitar fingerboard. By placing a number on the appropriate line, the string and fret of any note can be indicated. For example:

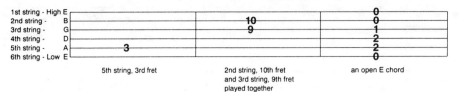

1st string - High E
2nd string - B
3rd string - G
4th string - D
5th string - A
6th string - Low E

5th string, 3rd fret

2nd string, 10th fret
and 3rd string, 9th fret
played together

an open E chord

Definitions for Special Guitar Notation

BEND: Strike the note and bend up ½ step (one fret).

BEND: Strike the note and bend up a whole step (two frets).

BEND AND RELEASE: Strike the note and bend up ½ (or whole) step, then release the bend back to the original note. All three notes are tied; only the first note is struck.

PRE-BEND: Bend the note up ½ (or whole) step, then strike it.

PRE-BEND AND RELEASE: Bend the note up ½ (or whole) step, strike it and release the bend back to the original note.

UNISON BEND: Strike the two notes simultaneously and bend the lower note to the pitch of the higher.

VIBRATO: Vibrate the note by rapidly bending and releasing the string with a left-hand finger.

WIDE OR EXAGGERATED VIBRATO: Vibrate the pitch to a greater degree with a left-hand finger or the tremolo bar.

SLIDE: Strike the first note and then with the same left-hand finger move up the string to the second note. The second note is not struck.

SLIDE: Same as above, except the second note is struck.

SLIDE: Slide up to the note indicated from a few frets below.

HAMMER-ON: Strike the first (lower) note, then sound the higher note with another finger by fretting it without picking.

PULL-OFF: Place both fingers on the notes to be sounded. Strike the first (higher) note, then sound the lower note by pulling the finger off the higher note while keeping the lower note fretted.

TRILL: Very rapidly alternate between the note indicated and the small note shown in parentheses by hammering on and pulling off.

TAPPING: Hammer ("tap") the fret indicated with the right-hand index or middle finger and pull off to the note fretted by the left hand.

NATURAL HARMONIC: With a left-hand finger, lightly touch the string over the fret indicated, then strike it. A chime-like sound is produced.

ARTIFICIAL HARMONIC: Fret the note normally and sound the harmonic by adding the right-hand thumb edge or index finger tip to the normal pick attack.

A.H. pitch: E

TREMOLO BAR: Drop the note by the number of steps indicated, then return to original pitch.

PALM MUTE: With the right hand, partially mute the note by lightly touching the string just before the bridge.

MUFFLED STRINGS: Lay the left hand across the strings without depressing them to the fret-board; strike the strings with the right hand, producing a percussive sound.

PICK SLIDE: Rub the pick edge down the length of the string to produce a scratchy sound.

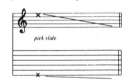

TREMOLO PICKING: Pick the note as rapidly and continuously as possible.

RHYTHM SLASHES: Strum chords in rhythm indicated. Use chord voicings found in the fingering diagrams at the top of the first page of the transcription.

SINGLE-NOTE RHYTHM SLASHES: The circled number above the note name indicates which string to play. When successive notes are played on the same string, only the fret numbers are given.